God Kept Me

A True Story of Surviving the Impossible in Times of War and Genocide

Puck Irambona

God Kept Me
Copyright © 2019 by Puck Irambona

ISBN 978-1-9990122-0-5

The quotes used in this book come from the New Living Translation (NLT) Bible, the New King James Version (NKJV) Bible, and the English Standard Version (ESV) Bible and are noted as such.

Contact us:

<u>**Niyipuck@yahoo.com**</u>

Editing and story development by:

StellarWork Editing
Natasha@stellarwork.info

Consultant in publication:

Kennedy Barasa Wanyonyi (Brilliant Breakthrough Solutions)
Kennedy.wanyonyi831@gmail.com

Cover design and page layout:

Jerry Mensah (J Mens Dreams Studios)
Jmens027@yahoo.com

Printed and assembled in Canada by:
DocuLink International, Ottawa, Ontario, Canada

Table of Contents

ACKNOWLEDGMENTS

My heartfelt thanks go out to everyone in my family for being there for me, for your comfort and for everything you have done for me.

I also want to thank the people who helped us in Kenya financially when life was tough.

In Canada, God gave us many parents, and I take this opportunity to thank the many families who received us as their own, adding us to the number of their children. I call their children my cousins. They may be white and I may be black, but we are family, and they will always hold a special place in my heart.

I also want to thank my spiritual parents, Pastors Ralph and Regina Dartey, for being there for my family. Thank you for every prayer you have prayed for us.

God bless you all.

INTRODUCTION

"But the Lord stood at my side and gave me strength, so that through me the message might be fully proclaimed and all the Gentiles might hear it. And I was delivered from the lion's mouth."
(2 Timothy 4:17 NIV)

Life is made up of the stories we tell. This book is the true story of my life.

When I came to Canada in 2006 and began telling people about what my siblings and I had been through, the response was absolute shock that we actually had those experiences. For most people, my story is like the ones we see in movies. As a result of the reactions I received from telling my story, I began to think of writing a book based on my life, to show just how far God has brought my family, and how He has kept us through it all.

We went from being wealthy and full of hope to being hopeless and near death, daily. With death at our doorstep time and again, we had no one to go to for support – only God. Only God remained in the picture through it all.

My intent for this book is to encourage and empower someone to look further than their current circumstances and find hope for their future through my story. If God could deliver my family from the hand of the enemy, then He can do it for anybody. Our God is able.

For 16 years of my life, I was one of the people you see in pictures carrying loads on their heads, not only struggling physically just to survive but also running for my life. You might not believe it based on how God has blessed me today, but yes, I was one of them. I once lived a life of terror, a life of danger – one that I wouldn't wish on anyone. My hope is that this book will lift someone's spirits and bring an understanding of what the Word of God reveals in Mark 9:23, when Jesus says, "If you can believe, all things are possible to him who believes."

CHAPTER 1
Born in Rwanda: Times of War and Genocide

"Behold, I am with you and will keep you wherever you go and will bring you back to this land; for I will not leave you until I have done what I have spoken to you."
(Genesis 28:14-15 NIV)

I was born in Rwanda, which is where my parents fled to from Burundi in 1972. During the war in Burundi, my grandfather was killed with his six sons. He was hiding in the bush, and after a while, rebels began calling out for people who were hiding, telling them the war was over and asking them to come out from behind the bush. That's when my grandpa came out. When they saw him, they wrapped him in a bag and beat him to death with the wooden side of a digging hoe.

That same year, my father was living in Nyakabiga, Bujumbura. One morning, he opened the window and saw many people with weapons. He tried to run, but they hit him in the head with the same type of gardening tool. Miraculously, my dad did not die. I remember when we were young, our father used to show us his scars. The war that was going on at that time in Burundi was so bad; this is the reason my parents fled to Rwanda.

Even in Rwanda, I grew up seeing war all around me. In 1992, we were living in the Mutara commune in Vyumba, Rwanda. I was four years old. That's when my elder siblings would take me with my friends to a sight-seeing place in the mountain to hear the guns being shot. As young children, we had no knowledge about what was going on; we went to that place just like were going to listen to music.

One morning, my family and I heard gunshots, and we went out of the house to see what was happening. Once outside, we saw the rebels shooting at everyone. We couldn't tell who they were, but they had different kinds of guns. My family was forced to flee, and we went in different directions.

A few of my siblings and I ended up hiding in a mountain with a group of people. As we were there, a man in our group turned on his flashlight to look for something, which caught the attention of a rebel who started shooting towards us. The gunshots didn't kill anyone in the crowd we were in; we were divinely protected.

When we arrived at home, we found our vehicle on fire. They had set the car on fire and pushed it against our house so that everyone and everything inside would burn with it.

During that year, the horrific war in Rwanda only escalated – the rebels kept attacking us, and we kept fleeing from them, mostly by hiding in the bushes. Every night we would run away from home and come back during the day. This was our reality.

CHAPTER 2
New Hope in the Capital City

"Indeed now, your servant has found favor in your sight, and you have increased your mercy which you have shown me by saving my life."
(Genesis 19:19 NKJV)

After a period fleeing from place to place in the village, my parents decided to move to Kigali, Rwanda. I was so happy to be moving. This meant we were leaving the village for the capital city. I didn't think of what we were leaving behind; I thought of the better life I was going to have.

In 1993, Melchior Ndadaye won the Burundian elections and became president of Burundi. Everyone thought that peace had finally come to our country. Because of this hope, my parents sent the children to Burundi to study, but a few months after the presidential election, the president was assassinated.

After that, the war in Burundi increased, and we couldn't think of what to do or where to go. We were only children living with our grandparents.

Our parents were in Rwanda at that time, and one day, to our great surprise, we saw our mother in sight. She was coming to take us back to Rwanda.

After a few months in Rwanda, the president of Rwanda, Juvénal Habyarimana was killed. It was 1994 – the year of the Rwandan genocide.

During this period, we spent a month in the house and ran out of food. The time came that my dad and big brother Richard had to go out to find food as we were going hungry. When they left the house, they walked with fear, not knowing if they would come back.

This was a time when we had witnessed our neighbors being burned in their house and others being shot right in front of us. On another occasion, we had stepped outside to the display of dead bodies on the ground. These were four people who had been chased, captured and hit with a piece of tree that they would trim and add nails to in order to use as a weapon to the head, resulting in the most horrendous scene.

God kept my father and brother during their trip to go find food. Despite the mass slaughter happening around them, and they eventually came back home safely.

Then one morning, people with guns came by our house looking for men to pick up and load the dead bodies to be thrown in the dumpster. My older sister went straight to my father to tell him to hide. Because she did this, they chased my sister and kept her for a while. But somehow, by divine intervention, she ended up finding favor in their sight, and they let her go. Soon after this incident, my dad told us to pack our bags, and we left. This time we were headed to the Democratic Republic of Congo – everyone except for my sister Georgette, who was visiting our Aunt in another province in Rwanda. Georgette ended up following our Aunt to a refugee camp in Tanzania while the rest of our family escaped to Congo.

CHAPTER 3
The Democratic Republic of Congo

*"But the Lord was with Joseph and showed him
mercy, and He gave him favor in the sight of the
keeper of the prison."*
(Genesis 39:21 NKJV)

Moving to the Democratic Republic of Congo was
the beginning of yet another chapter in our lives.
However, we had no idea of the danger we would be
running into.

On our journey to Congo, my family and I first
arrived at one location, and people with guns stopped
us and said, "Now is the time to kill." We were sure
that we were about to die. Then one of the gun
carriers mentioned that there were people hiding in
the building next to where we were. They suddenly
started shooting at the apartment, and we were
terrified. They killed many people in that building in
front of our very eyes. Yet again, the Lord's hand was
upon us, and we left that area untouched.

As we reached another location, other people with
guns pulled on my siblings, and my mother begged
the rebels to let them go. At the same moment, we
saw other rebels coming towards us with knives full
of blood. I thought that this time, it was surely over

for my family. How much more could we escape from?

At this point, the Lord was showing me that His heavenly protection is undeniable, because we escaped another bullet and they let us go without any harm. It's truly a wonder we made it out alive.

So we continued on our way to Congo with Jehovah Shammah – *The Lord is there* – undoubtedly by our side.

Once we arrived there, life was difficult. There were no jobs and no source of income. So we went to live in the Kagunga refugee camp. Sickness and diseases of all kinds increased because of the poor food quality and unhealthy environment. We lived in tents throughout this period in the refugee camp; we were 13 people plus our parents in one small tent. The food was provided by the United Nations, and we ate the same food repeatedly. The only food being provided was what we call "fufu" and beans. The food was not cooked; we were responsible to prepare the food, and we had to go from bush to bush looking for wood to cook with. The uncooked food would make us sick, and we had very few toilets in the whole camp. We had to line up for the washrooms, and it was tough to wait, especially at night. We had no shoes, and we had to go inside of these filthy washrooms. We also stepped on feces because many times people would have no choice but to relieve themselves wherever there was an empty spot. On top of that, we had no water to clean ourselves. In order to take a shower, we had to wait for it to rain because we couldn't afford to lose water. Until this day, I don't know how we survived these living conditions.

Schooling was important to my parents, and they wanted us to attend school. But in the refugee camp, we had no access to schools. All we did in the refugee camp was sit, wait for food, cook, eat and sleep. My father and other men were tired of eating the same food and not being able to do anything. Therefore, they decided to go hunt for food. While hunting, they killed birds and goats, and that was the meat we ate for months.

Many women in the refugee camp were raped, and some of them had children who sadly didn't know their fathers. As it is written in God's Word, it is the enemy who comes to steal, to kill, and to destroy (John 10:10). Just as I could see God's hand of protection throughout my journey and His goodness and mercies toward me, I also learned very quickly in life just how evil our enemy is.

During our time in the refugee camp, some Congolese men who had money approached my father and offered to pay him money for his daughters. My father responded, "I would rather die of hunger than give my daughters away." However, because of our living conditions with so many children living in one tent, our father proposed that my oldest sister Faida get married to her old friend from Burundi, to decrease the number of people in the tent. Faida agreed, got married and later moved to another refugee camp in another province.

Since 1996, we have lost touch of our sister Faida Sibonkomezi, her husband and their children. Faida left the Kagunga refugee camp to get married, and she and her husband moved to the Kashusha refugee camp. I don't know if she is still alive today. I continue to pray that someone knows where they are and will let our family know.

CHAPTER 4
From Congo to Burundi

Because life in the Congo refugee camp was so painful, my family and I left Congo for Burundi. Once we arrived in Burundi, we settled in Kumusenyi, Bubanza. For the first few months, we had nothing; we had to beg for food. As a result, my parents worked hard and started a business. This is when our lives began to improve, and we got a taste of what joy and peace was like.

A short time after, we began to hear gunshots surrounding the area. During the shooting spree, people were killed, but we were ok. A few days later, we heard rumors that our area would be attacked that night and people began to escape. People in our city packed and fled, and we did the same.

We ran to the mountains and camped there for three months. During these three months, we thought we had no chance of survival. We were expecting to die day and night. One day, the rebels attacked our campsite and took all the boys. They took my older brothers Richard and Eric to aid the insurgents fight and kill the innocent people.

In the campsite, we had no food and sickness was all around us. My sister Georgette, whom my mom had brought back from Tanzania to be with us, was struck by a terrible disease, and because of the lack of medication, she got very ill. Four men mistook my sister's body for a corpse and took her to the hospital. Once there, the doctors were able to treat her and by God's grace – by His hand of healing and deliverance – she survived.

When Georgette was taken to the hospital, our parents made the decision to move again and find another place to stay. They decided to move us to Mugara, Rumonge in Burundi.

At this time, my brother Richard escaped the rebels and informed us that our other brother Eric was not able to survive and was murdered.

In the end, my parents felt that we could no longer stay in Burundi because we could not keep changing cities and therefore keep changing schools. Everywhere we moved to in Burundi there was war. Consequently, my parents decided to go back to Congo and give it a second try.

CHAPTER 5
Another Try in the DRC

"You are my hiding place; You shall preserve me from trouble; You shall surround me with songs of deliverance. Selah"
(Psalm 32:7 NKJV)

This time in the Democratic Republic of the Congo, we did not go to the refugee camp. We went to the city of Uvira. Our parents had friends who had businesses there, and our parents helped them run their businesses. We were so happy that for two years there were no gunshots.

Then one day in 1996, people we did not know came close to where we were and began shooting in every direction. So we took some of our stuff, and we ran.

My mom had a small baby, my little sister Guilene, but she couldn't feed her; she didn't have enough breast milk because she was hungry as well. We did not have anything substantial to eat for days. We were only drinking water from the Tanganyika Lake and eating mangoes. The water was not clean at all; we could see blood in the water from the people who were killed and thrown into the lake. The baby got very ill from the dirty water, but the protected her and she survived.

Then we ran to Bubembe. On our way there, there were so many gunshots that we could not see the people who were shooting. When we finally arrived at a safe spot, we were so tired. For that reason, we decided to stop and sleep.

Early the next morning, the rebels came to where we were. We were terrified. They told us to go back to Uvira. So we went ahead of them, and they were shooting their guns in the air behind us. By the special grace of God, none of us got hit.

As we arrived at another location, one group of rebels told us to stop. We were afraid because we were the only ones they stopped. And to our surprise, they killed a goat and cooked it for us. We were incredibly hungry. So we ate, and we were happy.

What we didn't know, however, was that they were doing this for us because one of their leaders liked my sister. After we ate, they approached my mom and told her that they wanted my sister. My mom started to cry and told them that she could not let them take her. She said to them that if they took my sister, they would have to take her too.

They got angry and began yelling at us. Then they began to contemplate what bringing my mom would entail, and after making us hang around awhile, they let us go. Once more, we saw the hand of God upon our lives that day. And we kept going towards Uvira.

When we got to Uvira, we spent only one night there, and my parents decided to go back to Burundi. On our way back to Burundi, we heard people saying that all the men were being killed at the Burundian border. For that reason, my dad took some of my mom's clothes and dressed himself up like a woman. His strategy seemed to work, and nothing happened to him. This occurred in 1996, during the war in Congo.

CHAPTER 6
Back to Burundi

"For we do not wrestle against flesh and blood, but against principalities, against powers, against the rulers of the darkness of this age, against spiritual hosts of wickedness in the heavenly places."
(Ephesians 6:12 NKJV)

This time in Burundi, life was amazing. Our parents opened a Fanta business in the community. The neighbors were jealous because we had a fantastic experience at that moment.

Then one day, the man who provided milk for us to feed my little sister began to give us milk mixed with water. My older brother went to see the milkman and informed him that we knew what he was doing.

The man became furious, and several months later, he planned to kill my brother. Since witchcraft is a common practice in most African countries, his line of attack was to send evil spirits to my brother. So he did just that, and sickness hit my brother.

The first day my brother was sick, he couldn't move; on the second day, he got worse; and on the third day, we took him to the hospital. After receiving treatment, he began to vomit blood, something we had never seen in our entire lives. Then on the fourth day, while my brother rested in my arms, God took him home.

On the day before my brother passed away, my mom saw that there was no way he was going to make it. For two days, he was not speaking; nor was he eating. So, she said, "My son, I see your sickness isn't disappearing; repent, ask for forgiveness, and receive Jesus as your Lord and savior." Amazingly, he woke up and said, "Mother, thank you. To whomever I have caused wrong, I ask for forgiveness, and whomever did me wrong, I also forgive them. I repent and receive Jesus into my heart." After saying these words, he asked for food, he ate, and he began to tell us who was killing him and why. He told us that the man who was providing milk for our little sister had cursed him. My brother informed my mother that the milkman did this to him out of anger for confronting him about the milk being mixed with water. He said that God was showing him these things in the spirit realm.

Then my brother asked our mother to pray for him, saying that he was going to die. After she prayed, he began to shout, "Jesus is here! Jesus is here!" And those were his last words. He passed away on July 12, 1997.

CHAPTER 7
New Year's Day 1998 – A Day I Will Never Forget

"The thief does not come except to steal, and to kill, and to destroy. I have come that they may have life, and that they may have it more abundantly."
(John 10:10 NKJV)

On January 1st, 1998, we heard gunshots all over the city. Usually the soldiers in the city would shoot in the air, as a kind of farewell to the year just passed. The gunshots increased, but it didn't bother us because we were accustomed to it. In the morning time, we got dressed, prepared ourselves and went to church. When we arrived at church, it was closed, so we went back home. Around 9:00am the gunshots became too much. We began to think that this was not what we thought it was, but we couldn't confirm it. In a few minutes, we saw people with their guns running towards us, saying that we should start walking. I was nine years old at the time. We didn't know what was happening, but we marched with them. After about a half an hour, they stopped us, put us to the side, and asked my mother for her ID. My mother then sent my older sister back home to get the documents. They didn't wait for her to come back, however; we just kept walking.

We arrived at one location, and my mother held the hands of two of my siblings, with another one following in the back, and the three of them went to hide themselves. I was behind with my niece and two other siblings and didn't realize we were not with our mother anymore. Mom knew what was about to happen next, but we didn't know what was happening.

The rebels took us to a place where there were no houses; there were only trees and sand. They commanded the men to sit apart from the women and children. Then they told the women to take off their clothing and give it to them. Some people were naked because they didn't have any garments under their clothes. The rebels took the clothing and tied up the men, two by two. We saw them starting to hit the men on the head with different tools and weapons. After witnessing this, the people on the women and children side began to flee. The rebels chased us and whoever was caught was killed. Ahead of me was my friend Muhoza. She was hit with a long hammer, and the insides of her head popped right out. She never got up; she died on the spot.

My big sister was holding on to my little sister's hand but let her go without realizing it. I ended up finding myself with my niece and my little sister.

In all our surroundings the rebels were killing people. So I held the hands of my sister and my niece, and we marched towards the people who had weapons. Someone was standing like he was giving directions and commands. I asked him to have mercy on us and protect us. He responded by saying, "Don't worry, we will protect you."

Then they took us to a spot in the bushes and asked us to sit down while they kept bringing in more people. I don't know the exact number, but I'm sure there were more than 20 people. After a while, they took a rope and said they were going to tie us. They tied our wrists to one another and said they were doing so to prevent us from running away.

After tying us, they asked us to lay down with our bellies on the ground. While we were lying down, some of the people with weapons began to sing. This is the song they were chanting: "MANA, MANA, KORA IBITANGAZA VYAWE." The English meaning of the song was, "God, God, do your miracles." This song was like a signal for them to start killing the people because after they sang the song, they began hitting people on the head. To me, the song was like a voice telling me, "You're dead."

I couldn't even think of getting up because I was seeing so many people who were now dead. As a result, they hit me six times in the head. My sister was hit four times, and I'm not sure about my niece. While they were hitting me in the head with a gardening hoe, I raised my hand trying to cover my head but wasn't strong enough. Consequently, they hit my finger, and the skin was separated from the bones. Later, my finger was cut off.

Every time I look at my missing finger, I see proof of the God who protected me during this period of my life. If I didn't raise my hand over my head, I surely would have died, but God used His own ways to protect me. I also could have been traumatized by the experience, to the point of losing my mind. But this missing finger helps me praise the Lord for His deliverance. I give thanks to the Lord for saving my life; I may have lost a finger, but I am still alive.

After a while in those bushes, my friend Yves woke up, looked around, and saw that the rebels had left. He whispered to me, "Puck, get up. They are gone. Let's run." And he ran while I looked around for my sister and niece to see if everything was well with them. My niece was crying a lot. I tried to hold her arm, but she would not get up. I woke up my sister, and she was able to stand. There was no time to think, so we followed Yves and left my niece behind.

My sister couldn't run; she kept falling and not being able to pick herself up, but I couldn't leave her. Because we marched so slowly, the rebels found us again. They came running to us and said, "Lie down." We asked them to have mercy on us, but before we could finish our sentence, they gave us more strikes to the head. They hit my sister once and hit me twice, and we spent hours on the ground not knowing where we were.

After a while, I stood up and looked at my sister, and I realized it was impossible to carry her. I couldn't transport her, and she couldn't walk. I looked at her with sadness and told her, "Bye my sister; we will meet again if it is God's will."

I left with sorrow in my heart leaving my little sister behind. I thought she was the only one I had left, that everyone else was dead. After everything that transpired, I didn't know if anyone in my family was still alive. So I entered the bushes, not knowing where I was heading.

I had severe bleeding dripping from my head and my right arm. My left arm was numb due to the way it was tied.

I arrived at a spot that had prickly grass, and I sensed in my heart that if I entered those bushes, I would survive. Nobody was going to look for me there because it would hurt. Therefore, I went to the spikey bush and spent about three hours lying there. It was excruciating but I didn't pay attention to the pain because I didn't know if I would survive.

When I came out, I saw a farm in the forest with Cassava trees, and I went there. I spent about an hour sitting in that forest not knowing what to do.

Then I remembered someone once telling me that a person could die from bleeding excessively. I thought to myself, "I am bleeding too much." So, I took leaves and placed them on my head and on my hand to try to stop the bleeding. Then I began to drink my own blood. I did not want to die; I was willing to do anything to save my own life.

During this time, those who were killing people kept passing by me, but they couldn't see me because I was hiding. I could see them, but they couldn't see me. I was bleeding all day and did not eat a thing. In the evening, I was thinking of how I would sleep in this large forest by myself, but I knew in my heart that God would be there with me.

It was starting to get dark when suddenly, I heard the voice of a small child calling from a distance; she was calling the name of our neighbor's child. An inner voice told me to follow the child's voice and find the child before night-time. At that moment I had forgotten about the rebels I had seen walking around. I didn't even think about what could happen if I came across them again.

I stood up and walked towards the sound of the child crying out; she didn't stop until I got to her.

When I got to the child, I discovered that it was my sister Florence whom I had left behind. At that moment, I remembered what I had told her: that we would meet again, God willing. And the Lord is so faithful and kind that when we call on Him, He is there, and He answers. Words cannot describe how happy I was to see my sister. It was a miracle. I forgot all the physical pain I was in and started to take care of my little sister.

I asked her if she had seen my niece Lice and she said no. Then we continued on our way; we didn't know where we were headed, but we kept going.

My sister soon got very tired and hungry. She started crying for water, but there was no water to give her. So I told her to go on my back. I couldn't hold her hand because my hands were numb.

As we continued walking, we saw people with children sitting together outside. We joined them and stayed with them all night. When it was time to sleep, however, we couldn't find rest because of the mosquitoes. We asked the people who were there for something to cover ourselves with, but they refused. They didn't want blood on their clothing. Consequently, we took off our clothes and covered our heads to prevent the mosquitos from biting our open wounds.

In the morning, the people we were with said that they were going back to their homes. We wanted to go with them but my new friend Gilbert, whom I had met that morning, suggested that we go to the Gatumba refugee camp instead. He wanted to see what was going on around us. I listened to him and didn't follow the others.

Gilbert and I went to stand on a hill to see what was happening to our homes. From up high, we saw the people we were going to follow who had refused to give us clothes to cover ourselves. They were being killed right in front of our eyes. I thank God we didn't follow them. Once again, the Lord intervened, and we didn't die that day.

Afterwards, Gilbert, my sister and I left that area to go to the Gatumba refugee camp. We saw too many people who were killed and others who were still alive but could not walk or move.

Then we met another group of people, and we walked with them. As we were going about our way, two rebels came out of the bushes with guns. We were about 10 people, and all of us began running in different directions. My sister was behind me, and I told myself that I was not going to leave her again. While other people were running, I stopped and waited for my sister. I shouted, "Folo! Folo! Come!" and we ran away together.

By God's mercy and favor, they did not catch us, and our lives were spared once again.

My friend Gilbert ended up going in another direction, and now it was just my sister and me. With nobody around, we didn't know where to go. In all of our surroundings, there were dead bodies. These are images I will never forget.

We passed by many people who died, but the death of two men made me especially sad. One of them was killed like a goat. They took him, hung him upside down, removed all the skin from his body and left him to die. Every time I remember that man, I cannot believe human beings can do something like that. As for the other man, he had all of his clothes removed, was cut all over his body and was also left to die. We were too young to have witnessed such gruesome acts, and it was troubling even to try to understand how a human being could do such a thing to another human being. We were young but what we saw will never leave our memories.

At this point, we began to ask ourselves what we would do next. We saw a man coming, so we waited and walked along with him. There was nothing else to do but to follow him. At one point, he wanted us to pass where two rebels were; we were so afraid, but we followed him. When we arrived at the spot, we saw the dead bodies of two men who were with us before running away from the rebels. We told the man that we were sorry, but we could not keep going that way.

Florence and I took another direction with gunshots all around us. It was a vast forest; we were terrified, but we eventually arrived at an area where we could see the houses. So we kept going and we saw a man who was eating under an avocado tree. I told my sister, "Let us go quickly so that we can ask him for something to eat." We couldn't walk too fast since we were tired. It was our second day without eating, and we were bleeding. And when we finally got to where the man was, he was done eating. By this time, we were terribly hungry and exhausted, but we had no choice but to keep going so that we could get out of that forest. Much too often we would see a house in front of us, thinking we were close to being done walking, relieved that finally, we were going to rest. Yet when we would arrive, nobody would be around, and we had to keep going; this seemed to never end.

Finally, I told my sister that we had to go in one of the houses so that we could rest. We opened the first house and saw blood everywhere. When we looked around, we saw a man and a woman with children who had been killed. We were so afraid; we also realized that the killers were still there. We didn't know what to do so we kept going. We walked extremely fast to leave that place.

We saw so many people who were killed and others who needed help, but there was no help and nothing we could do for them. I don't know if these people survived or not but to this day, I think about them, hoping they also got a chance to see their silver lining.

Florence and I continued walking, and we saw houses again, but this time there were many people walking around outside. We felt very happy to see people again. We started to forget about dying; our courage came back and our enthusiasm as well. Yet, nobody from that group could help us. They felt sorry but would not even give us water to drink. So we started asking people if they could show us where the hospital was. They provided us with very vague directions, but no one made the effort to help in any real way. I felt so sad to see many people who were able but just didn't have the heart to help.

On the road searching for the hospital, we met someone who knew us, and he told us that our mother and father were killed. I was not shocked because I couldn't imagine how they would survive all I had witnessed. He then showed us where the Catholic Church was, and we went there.

The nuns at the Catholic Church were amazing; they took care of many survivors. I was very grateful that the church was there because we needed to rest, and it helped to see more survivors like us. I think of them even now, and hope they are blessed wherever they are. Although the nurses were able to give us medication, we didn't receive anything to eat. And we were almost at the end of our second day without food. After giving us the medication, the nuns started talking to us, asking questions about what had happened, and what we saw. They took pictures and videos of us. After a few hours there, they took us to the Prince Regent Charles hospital.

When we got to the hospital, we were given more medication. And I began to cry. The two men who were treating me asked me why I was crying. When I told them I was hungry, one of them said, "Do you see your mom here? Go tell your mom that you are hungry." I stopped crying right away. Then they cut my injured finger and took me in one of their rooms.

In the morning, they transferred us to another hospital called Roi Khaled. When we arrived there, I started thinking about how we could leave. I was hungry; it was our third day without food. I also knew that one of our uncles lived close by.

While I was thinking of leaving, I saw people arriving at the hospital looking for people they knew.

So I looked to see if I knew any of them. That's when I saw my mom and sister Dina passing by; they did not see us, or maybe they didn't recognize us because we had bandages all over. I shouted, "Mommy, Mommy!"

I had been told that my parents were killed and there my mom was, right in front of me. I was so happy to know that we were not alone – our mother and sister were there. My mom looked at us and started crying. I hugged her and told her that my niece Lice had died, and my mother informed me they had also killed my father. I learned later that they killed my dad by cutting his head in half with a machete.

Then our mom went to buy food. She bought us fruits and other food, and we ate. I don't understand how we survived three days without eating, especially while we were bleeding and walking long distances. Our God is good; He saved our lives. I will always love Him because He has shown me that He has a good plan for our lives.

We ended up being kept at the hospital for six months, and I stayed home one year without going to school. When I left the hospital, I got sick again and had to go back to the hospital for treatment.

Mom took care of nine children alone after the death of our father and four of our siblings, as well as the disappearance of our sister Faida and her family in Congo.

My Sister Dina

At the end of year in 1998, my sister Dina was selling clothes in her clothing store. She was earning lots of money. One day she woke up and told us that she was going to get money from her employees. Dina had a one-year-old daughter who usually stayed with everyone else at home while she went to work. But on that day, she took her daughter with her because she was going to visit a friend afterward.

She left home early in the morning, and she did not come back. Mom tried to look for her everywhere but could not find her. She even visited all the prisons of Burundi.

We heard from people who said they saw her in a police car, but they didn't know where they were taking her. Others told us that they saw her being killed.

We finally learned that she was killed because her employee wanted to take over her business. The employee told the police that Dina was working with the rebels and they killed her without even investigating or putting her into prison. They murdered her, and the baby was thrown into the Tanganyika Lake.

CHAPTER 8
My Mother Goes to Jail

After the war in Rukaramu, in rural Bujumbura, we resided in Gatumba, Bujumbura but our mom continued to run her business in Rukaramu. She would work in Rukaramu and come home afterwards.

In 2001, we saw the police coming to our house looking for our mom, but she was not home. They entered our house by force, searching everywhere, checking the papers. We didn't know what was happening; we were terrified to see what they were doing.

In the evening we waited, but our mom didn't come home. The following day, we heard in the news that our mother was in jail. She was put in prison because they thought she was involved in a plane incident that had happened just the year before when a plane full of people was shot down in Rukaramu – where mom was doing business at the time. Because of her wealth and status, they thought she and other prominent people were responsible for shooting down the plane. This Sabena plane crash was all over the news in the year 2000.

It was heartbreaking for the family to have our mother taken away from us. It was a real tragedy because now we had no parents to provide for us. My younger brother Orest, who was only three at the time, stayed with us for a few days and then mom asked the officials if she could bring him to the prison to stay with her. They agreed, and my little brother joined my mother in the prison.

Life soon became hard and confusing for our family again. We had to ask the neighbors for food. Some of them were very nice to us, and others ignored us. But my mother never forgot about her children. Whenever we visited her in prison, she would give us her leftovers. At every meal, she kept food for us, and when we went to visit her, she would provide us with the food.

One day, the landlord came over and informed us that he would be coming to the house in a few days and that he didn't want us to be there. He was trying to be careful about kicking us out. We hadn't been able to pay rent in two months. We couldn't blame our landlord, but at the same time, there was no understanding. So we left Gatumba, Bujumbura and went to live in Kumusenyi, Bubanza.

Before my mother went to prison, she bought some land in Kumusenyi, and she was in the process of building a house. The house was like a mansion; it was vast and beautiful, but it was not entirely finished. The windows were not covered, and there were no doors. We had to place plastic bags and cardboard boxes around the house so we could have privacy.

During the night we put heavy materials against the doors and windows so no one could try and come in. My relatives were living in that house before we moved in. We had cousins living there, and when we arrived, we were happy because we were with people we knew.

Then one day as we were sleeping, we felt someone pulling our legs. I screamed, and he ran. We couldn't sleep all night after that. Later that morning we began to investigate who that person was, and we found out it was our neighbor. We never bothered to ask him about it, and that was the end of that.

CHAPTER 9
Our Mother Comes Home

"About midnight Paul and Silas were praying and singing hymns to God, and the other prisoners were listening to them. Suddenly there was such a violent earthquake that the foundations of the prison were shaken. At once all the prison doors flew open, and everyone's chains came loose."
(Acts 16:25-26 NIV)

Seven months had passed since our mom went to prison and brought our little brother Orest with her. The seventh month was her last, as there was an ongoing investigation about the case which we weren't aware of, and they came to find out that she was innocent.

One day, to our great surprise, our mother came home. We ran and hugged her; this was the first time we saw her outside of the prison in seven months. She told us she was not returning to jail; it was the happiest day of our lives.

We had our mom back. We had our hero again. In the seven months she was in prison she gained lots of insight and understanding about life, and most importantly, she grew in her faith.

While my mom was in prison, people came to her speaking French, and they asked her to sign papers. She couldn't speak French, but she signed the papers and was very excited because she thought she was signing papers for her release. My sister Georgette came to visit her after that, and it was announced that my mom would be released the next day. They rejoiced together. The next day, Georgette went to get her from prison, and when she arrived, mom wasn't there.

She looked everywhere but couldn't find her. She asked the officials where she was, and they told her she was transferred into the big prison of Burundi. My sister wept and wept.

We went to see our mother in that prison, and it was maximum security; we couldn't even give her a hug. We could only speak to her through a glass wall. It was very emotional for us seeing her like that. My brother who was in jail with my mom was still too young to be interested in coming to look at his siblings.

When she was transferred to that prison, all hope was lost. There was no getting her back, and she was also aware of that. While she was in there, she began to pray and started a bible study group. Sometimes we would go see her, and she would be busy teaching a bible study group. She was committed to teaching the

Word of God, and she gained so much from it. My mom was always a believer but not a firm believer and being in prison transformed her life. I believe she just couldn't bear the thought of her children suffering outside of the prison. She got to a place where God was all she had left, and she turned to Him as her only hope.

It was a few months later that she was found innocent and having her come back home was absolutely the workings of God.

CHAPTER 10
Our Mother Prospers in the Land

"Then Isaac sowed in that land, and reaped in the same year a hundredfold, and the Lord blessed him. The man began to prosper, and continued prospering until he became very prosperous."
(Genesis 26:12-13 NKJV)

My mom had a business before going to prison, but she lost everything by the time she came out. Therefore, she went to the bank to ask for a loan, and she was approved. They trusted her because she had worked with the bank before and was well known there.

So my mom opened a bar. In this bar, however, there were no alcoholic beverages. My mom chose not to serve alcohol because she was serious about God and the Bible and didn't want to lead other people astray. Nevertheless, her business became very successful, and she began to work on the house.

We were able to add metal windows, metal doors, and it finally became a home. My mom even began to build more houses beside it, and before we knew it, there were three tenants renting our apartments. My mom became very wealthy and was looking to expand her business beyond the bar. She acquired lands, planted rice, and rented houses all over Burundi. And she built all of that in only two years. Somehow, she was able to manage all those businesses.

During this time, all the children were attending school. School mattered to our mom, even though she dropped out of grade six. After school, the girls would take care of the bar while she traveled and took care of the rest.

My mother had a good heart; she wanted everyone to succeed. And with all her success, she felt terrible that her brothers had nothing. So she also provided for her brothers living in the village.

One day she went to see her mother and brothers and proposed that one of her brothers come start a business with her help and guidance. My uncle Gabriel came and began a business, and it became successful.

This was all during mom's first year out of prison. It reminds me of the story of King Nebuchadnezzar, in which God fulfilled the kingdom in just twelve months: "Twelve months later, as the king was walking on the roof of the royal palace of Babylon…" (Daniel 4:29 NIV), as well as the story of Isaac who sowed in the land and reaped a hundred folds that same year. The Lord blessed him, and he became very prosperous (Genesis 26:12-13). The same way He did for King Nebuchadnezzar and Isaac, the Lord established my mother's life – all in one year.

During the time my mom prospered in the land, the war was still taking place, but it was not severe. Even so, we were always ready to run.

CHAPTER 11
The Passing of Our Mother

"Jesus said to her, 'I am the resurrection and the life. The one who believes in me will live, even though they die; and whoever lives by believing in me will never die.' Do you believe this?"
(John 11:25-26 NIV)

On September 9, 2003, I was very ill. I was throwing up and had a very high fever. I couldn't sleep by myself because I was sick, so I went to go sleep with mom around 9:00pm. I found my younger siblings in bed with her so I didn't stay there, for I would be sleeping on the floor. So I asked her to pray for me before I went to sleep.

I returned to my bedroom that night not knowing that my mom's prayer would be the last words she would ever speak to me. If I knew at that moment that this was the last time I would ever be with my mom, I would have gladly slept on the floor. But I didn't.

An hour after leaving my mom's room, we began to hear gunshots; we could make out that they were far away, so we were not concerned. Then we heard them getting closer. And usually, by the time the shots were this close, we had to get out and run. That day, however, we didn't run, which was unusual for us.

Mom told everyone to hide under the bed and not move. She stayed in the room with my sister Florence and my niece Uwizeye who was just visiting; the rest came to hide in my room. The gunshots kept drawing nearer, and before we knew it, people were hitting on our door and screaming. The door was metal, so it was not the easiest to break down. After many attempts, mom surrendered, knowing they wouldn't leave without getting what they came for.

In many neighborhoods all around the country, people called my mother, "Mama Richard." They loved and respected her as their own mother, and the name caught on. Almost everyone knew who Mama Richard was.

When mom surrendered to the men at the door, she said, "It's me, Mama Richard. I'm coming to open the door." After opening the door for them, they began slapping her, kicking her, and spitting in her face. She begged them for mercy, but they didn't listen to her. My sister Florence and niece Uwizeye couldn't let go of our mom, so they took them together.

When my mom opened the door, they began to search the bedroom. I was under the bed with the rest of my siblings. We held our breath because we couldn't risk being heard. Some men came into the room and took clothing and everything that was valuable.

Shortly after they left, our neighborhood night watchers came to our house and knocked on the door. We were too afraid to open the door. Therefore we stayed quiet. They ended up shouting our names, and I recognized their voices. So I went to open the door, and they took us somewhere outside to sit and wait until everything calmed down. We sat in that spot for the whole night. Blankets were brought to us so that we could rest, but there was no way we could sleep after that.

My mother, sister, and niece were all gone, so there was no way we could rest nor sleep. We waited till morning, and my uncle Gabriel was there. We had completely forgotten that he lived in the house with us, so I asked him how he found us. He explained that when the rebels came, he had covered himself in his bed and no one saw him. And after the night watchers came to get us, they had also grabbed him. He also told us that while he was walking to a safe place, a rebel almost shot him. He showed us the spot on the tip of his ear where the bullet just nicked him. It was only a small mark as the bullet barely touched him.

Then went back home hoping to see our mother. When we arrived at the house, people came by and told us that our mom was murdered. I ran to see where she was, and I found her body under a big tree. They had shot her on the chest and in the mouth.

I asked people who were around me to help me to take her home. When we arrived home, I warmed up the water, and the women who were there with me washed her. Next, we covered her with a blanket. I will never forget the image of my mom, of where she was sitting, and how she looked after being killed.

Currently there was a big crowd of people surrounding our house. I wasn't really paying attention, but the number of people was astonishing. While we were there, my uncle Cyprien Nsengiyumva, who was living in the city, came and started taking charge of the situation. He arranged for transportation to move the body of my mother out of the city.

Our uncle continued taking care of everything concerning my mom's funeral and sacrificed everything to be there for us. He was supposed to leave to go join his family in South Africa the next day, but he postponed it all to stay in Burundi with us.

The death of our mother meant that we were orphans, and that was a frightening feeling. We went to bury our mother, and on our way there I could only hear the horns. I couldn't see anything. My family was doomed from this moment on; this is what I thought to myself. What would happen next? Everything we had was taken from us. How in the world were we going to survive? Only God knew.

When we arrived at the burial site, people were singing, and they put her in the ground. At that moment I realized that everything I cared about was leaving my sight forever.

As soon as she was buried, we began to hear gunshots. There were countless people at the burial site, and they all rushed back to their cars. And that was it. I had said goodbye to my mother. Today I understand that while I said bye to her at that moment, heaven had received a great treasure.

CHAPTER 12
No Longer Orphans

"I will not leave you orphans; I will come to you."
(John 14:18 NIV)

Next was the decision about where each child would go, and they began to separate us. One of my uncles chose my brothers because he was convinced that taking girls would lead to having more children. He thought that the girls would get pregnant.

Then there was my uncle Cyprien, who had come to live with our family when he was young. He was in grade six when my mom took him in to stay with us. He was living with us when I was born, and when he finished his studies, he got married while at our home. He was like another child that God had given my parents. He was my uncle, but became like a brother, and at the end, he became like a father.

He ended up relocating to South Africa, but he moved to Burundi in 2001 with his wife and children. Life in Burundi was very tough for them. They were not used to hearing gunshots all the time. After one year, his wife returned to South Africa, and at the time of my mother's passing, he was getting ready to join his wife. But while everybody refused to take care of us, he called his wife and asked her if they could take care of us. His wife accepted, and we went to live with him. I really thank God for my uncle, whom I call the angel that God sent to help us. I also appreciate his wife for agreeing to take on seven children in addition to their own three at the time. It takes a specific type of woman to accept to take care of ten children. May the Lord reward her for her sacrifice.

During the war in Rwanda in 1994, my uncle Cyprien had gone with us to the Kagunga refugee camp in Congo. It was there that he decided to marry his childhood friend. After their wedding, they made the decision to go to the refugee camp in Tanzania.

Their time in Tanzania was tough and they did not stay there for long. They went to Zambia searching for a better life, but things were even harder there.

I remember one day our uncle telling us about his working conditions. Someone gave him a job to watch the chickens. It was a tough job because thieves with guns were always going there to steal the chickens. Instead of watching the chickens, those working this job were busy hiding themselves. One day, someone who was working with my uncle had a plan. He wanted to get their boss to see that there were thieves trying to kill them in order to steal the chickens. So, they agreed to start hitting each other hard so that they could show the bruises to their boss and blame the thieves. My uncle asked if he could start with the hitting and the other man agreed. So, my uncle took a stick and struck him. The man fell, and my uncle was afraid, thinking his coworker might get angry and kill him. When it was my uncle's turn to get hit, he ran away. In the morning, they followed through on their plan and told their boss about the thieves and showed him the bruises. Then the boss moved them and put them to work somewhere else.

Since the living conditions in Zambia were too difficult for them, they decided to go to South Africa. While they were in South Africa, they went to study to be evangelists. After their studies, they were sent to work in Burundi. We were so happy to have them come back to Burundi, but we didn't know God was also sending them back for us.

As mentioned before, they were not used to hearing gunshots every day. Every time they listened to the guns my uncle's wife would ask him to go back to South Africa. And it was after one year that my uncle's wife went back there. My uncle stayed in Burundi, but nobody knew why he stayed. Only God knew. He was always saying that he would be leaving in the next month, but somehow, he never went.

When they killed my mom, our uncle Cyprien was still in Burundi. He took us to his house, and we lived with him for six months. The Holy Bible says that

God is the father of orphans and the defender of the widows: "A father of the fatherless, a defender of widows, is God in His holy habitation." (Psalm 68:5 NKJV) We saw the hand of God on our family as He sent His angel – my uncle – to save our lives. If it wasn't for God and His preservation, I don't know where I would be. God could not let us continue to suffer; He had a good plan for us.

CHAPTER 13
From Kenya to Canada

"For I know the thoughts that I think toward you, says the Lord, thoughts of peace and not of evil, to give you a future and a hope."
(Jeremiah 29:11 NKJV)

My uncle could not see our future in Burundi. So he told us that we were going to Kenya. He knew that there were people there who could help us. He got all the documents we needed and took us to Kenya.

We lived in Kenya for two years and three months, and life was not easy. We were all living in one small house with one bedroom and a living room. My uncle slept in the living room, and seven of us shared a room. We were eating the same food because we had very little money. My uncle did everything he could to get us something to eat, and our auntie was sending us money; it just wasn't enough for all of us.

During our stay in Kenya, our uncle took us to the United Nations, where they began asking us about our experiences. They asked us how our parents and siblings were killed, and about the wars we experienced. For one year we met with them, answering all their questions about what had happened to us. They would meet with us separately in different rooms and do one-on-one interviews with each of us.

After one year, they told us that our file had been forwarded to the Canadian Embassy. While we were in Kenya, my uncle's wife moved to Canada, and she began the process of bringing her husband. My uncle ended up getting a visa to come to Canada. We were so happy because we knew one day we were going to move to Canada as well.

In many ways, we saw God at work in our lives in Kenya. After my uncle left for Canada, the UN started to give us money to live. Furthermore, a church in Kenya called Friends Church was paying our school fees.

CHAPTER 14
How We Got to Canada

"...And surely I am with you always, to the very end of the age."
(Matthew 28:20 NIV)

When we had first arrived in Kenya in March 2004, we didn't know anybody; all we knew was the UN. We stayed in a cheap hotel. We had some money from things we had sold in Burundi before traveling and were hopeful to survive a few months. We started going to the UN seeking resettlement, and it wasn't easy because we didn't know if they were going to help us due to their long waiting list. We had to wake up early in the morning in order to be at the front in line. We would spend all day there without eating, and we were hungry. A few months later, we were able to meet the agent who oversaw resettling people and families, and we finally got a chance to have an interview.

We were asked why we chose to go to the UN, and we told them that we had no other place to go. We could barely speak English, but they had someone to translating for us. We told them everything that happened to us, the struggles we faced in life from the time we were very young, that we had never lived

60

peacefully, and that we had lost our parents and siblings. Our story touched them and brought everyone to tears. After hearing our story, however, they didn't believe it completely. That is why they arranged one-on-one interviews with each of us, even including our youngest brother who was only six years old at that time. They asked him if it was true that our mom died or if we were making it up. They told him that they would give him a toy car if he told them the truth. My six-year-old brother told them that he saw our mom's dead body, and he opened his mouth to show them how my mom looked after she was shot in the mouth. My brother knew what had happened to our mom and he couldn't make up a story and lie; he was too young to be able to do that. He was young, but he told them what he had seen with his own eyes. When he came out of the interview, I asked him where he got the toy car, and said that he was asked to tell the truth in order to get a toy.

They interviewed each of us the same way, and we were very confident about what we were saying because we had all witnessed the same thing. We even had pictures of our mom's funeral to show to the UN agents.

We had interviews almost every two weeks for one year and a half. They would ask us the same questions repeatedly. We had pictures and a video of our mother's funeral and death certificates for both our parents. We also showed them what had happened to my sister Florence and me in 1998. You could still see the scars on our heads and where the rebels had cut my finger. We had many things to show them in order to prove to them that what we were saying had happened.

After a year of waiting, we began to lose patience, and life in Kenya wasn't perfect. We were living in a tiny house with one bedroom, a tiny living room, kitchen, and one bathroom. The seven of us were all sleeping in the same place. We were all using one bathroom. We had water once a week and had to keep it in big containers for it to last for the whole week. That was the water we would use to cook with, to shower with, and clean the toilet. It wasn't easy.

We were always waiting to hear good news from the UN, and what seemed like ages, nothing was happening.

In Nairobi, Kenya, we were attending a church called Friends Church, and they would give food to people in need on a monthly basis – food like corn flour, rice, beans and cooking oil, and the amount of food was given according to the number of people in the household. The church was also helping our family by paying the school fees for all the children for the two years we lived in Kenya. God blessed us through this church and opened many doors for our family.

In every situation we faced, God was with us and came through for us. We all went to school when many children stayed home because they couldn't afford to pay their school fees. As He promises in His Word, God never left us alone nor did He forget about us: "Be strong and courageous; do not be afraid or terrified of them, for it is the LORD your God who goes with you; He will never leave you nor forsake you." (Deuteronomy 31:6 NIV)

My uncle's wife and children ended up being accepted to come to Canada from South Africa. When my aunt moved to Canada, she sponsored our uncle, and he was able to join her within a few months. His time had come for him to join his family.

It is while he was waiting for his visa that we received a letter from the Canadian embassy inviting us for an interview. It was a very happy moment. We didn't know how the meeting was going to go if we were going to be accepted or not. My uncle was moving to Canada, and we were hopeful that one day we were going to join him. We were young but very smart, and we came up with the idea to go to the UN to tell them that our uncle was leaving and that we did not have money to survive. We are thankful to the UN and everything they did for us. They told us that they were going to give us money every month. They usually don't give out money, but they did it for us, and they checked up on us on a monthly basis to see how we were doing. My uncle had left, but the UN was there for us.

When we went for the interview with the Canadian Embassy, it was like they just wanted to see our faces; it felt like we were accepted into Canada before the meeting. The interview was brief and easy. When we finished the meeting, the beautiful lady who interviewed us said, "You are welcome to Canada." We were very shocked and happy at the same time. "Welcome to Canada!" We couldn't believe what we had heard. Usually, after the interview, people go home and await the confirmation letter informing them whether they were accepted, but for us, we knew we were approved the day of the interview. This was unheard of and could only be the favor of God.

A few months later we were sent to do medical exams and go learn about Canada. After that, we had to wait for our visas to arrive. Very often we would go check the list of people about to travel, would not see our names and would go home disappointed. One day, one of our friends told us that he saw us on the list. We were very excited. We went there, and it was true – our names were on the list. Finally, the day came for us to get ready to go to the airport.

We didn't have any money on us; however at the Nairobi airport, we met a few Chinese people who liked us and gave us thirty dollars. It was the first time we were about to go on an airplane, and we were thrilled!

When we got on the plane, we went to sit in business class; it was very welcoming and comfortable. Then one of the flight attendants came by and asked to see our tickets. We showed them to her, and she asked us to stand up.

We didn't understand what was happening. We couldn't speak English, but when the flight attendant understood that we were refugees, she showed us where to sit. In every airport that we stopped at there was someone waiting to show us where to go. When we got to London, England, we were so tired and hungry. We used the thirty dollars that the Chinese people had given us to buy something to eat. We had to wait for hours to take our next plane, but it didn't matter to us because we knew our days of suffering were almost over.

When we got to Edmonton, it was night-time, and nobody was there to receive us. We followed other people, but we didn't know where we were going. It was the middle of the night.

When we were in London, someone had called our uncle to tell him that our airplane was going to be late, but it was not. So we ended up sleeping on the chairs at the Edmonton airport. In the morning we asked people who were cleaning if anybody could help us. They asked us if we had a phone number they could call for us. We said no. Before leaving Kenya, we gave away everything we had. We didn't even have anything to write down the number with. Another cleaning person came by and asked us the same question – if we had a number he could call for us – and again, our answer was no. Then he said there was no other option than for us to go back to where we came from. This conversation was very hard for us as we were speaking broken English, but he could still understand some of what we were saying. We asked if he could understand French, but he could not.

Before leaving Kenya, one of our friends wrote a letter to someone, and he put the lady's number on the envelope. Suddenly we remembered that we had that letter. When we checked the message, there was a phone number on it. So we asked the cleaning person if he could call that number. We didn't know the lady whose number was on the letter, but we just told the man to call her. When he called, nobody picked up the phone. Then we heard him talking to himself; we didn't know he was leaving a message. He told us to wait and that they may call back. After a few minutes they called back, and by God's grace, the man was still there. He gave us the phone, and I talked to the lady on the line. She was Burundian, so I was speaking my language.

I asked her if she knew Cyprien Nsengiyumva, but she said no. Then she asked me the name of my uncle's wife. I told her, and the lady said, "Yes, I know her."

So the lady called my uncle's house and my uncle called social services. We didn't know anything about social services, but they arrived before my uncle and family. They talked to us like they knew us. They knew all of our names, and we were surprised. After a few minutes, my uncle and family arrived. We were so happy because now no one could take us back to Kenya.

We thought we were going to leave with my uncle, but we ended up leaving with the people from social services. We were brought to a place they called "reception". That is where the newcomers would go while waiting to be placed into a home. We ended up staying there for a month. They were helping us to get Canadian documents, teaching us how to do groceries and taking us to different places in Edmonton.

Many people came by to see us and helped us. The Catholic Church enabled us to connect with many people who assisted us. After three months in Canada, one of the families they connected us to became our family. Until now, they are still in our lives and their amazing children as well. They are my Canadian parents, and I will forever be grateful for all they have done for us and continue to do.

I would like to pause here and thank the Canadian Embassy for accepting us to come to this Country. I will never forget the beautiful lady who first welcomed us to Canada. When we arrived, the Canadian Embassy helped us financially for two years. I thank God for enabling us to come to this peaceful land. We have now been in Canada for twelve years; five of us are married, and two are going to University. Life here in Canada is lovely; I sleep without thinking of danger. There are no guns behind me, and I don't have to carry my clothes every day ready to run. I have peace of mind.

I also thank God for giving me a forgiving heart. After all that has happened to me, God has given me the strength and ability to forgive everyone who hurt me.

CHAPTER 15
The Passing of My Uncle Cyprien

It was May 11, 2014, on Mother's Day. We were so happy calling my uncle's wife to wish her a happy Mother's Day. On that day, the devil wanted to steal my joy. Around 10:00pm, I was getting ready to sleep, and someone called. We usually don't pick up the phone at that time, so I didn't answer. Then my husband's phone rang, but he didn't pick up either. After a few seconds, my phone rang again, so I told my husband that I had to answer the phone. So, I picked it up, and my sister was crying, "Uncle has died!" I said, "What?!" I could not believe my angel could go so soon. I asked her what had happened, and she explained that he had died in a car accident. I dropped the phone and started to cry.

I am lost for words to describe how thankful I am for the life of my uncle Cyprien and everything he did for our family. God will surely never forget everything he did for us. I know my uncle is with the Lord and one day we are going to see him again. I believe that, just as God sent my uncle to take care of us, He will also make sure that his wife and four children are taken care of as well. Just as God looked after us, He will undoubtedly look after my aunt and cousins. Rest in peace, my dear uncle.

Source: Marie-Goretti Niyakire

The following excerpt is taken from the Edmonton Journal article describing what happened to my uncle at the time of his passing.

Beloved pastor killed when his car was hit by detached trailer on Airport Road

By Alexandra Zabjek, Edmonton Journal
May 16, 2014

Cyprien Nsengiyumva, an immigrant from Burundi who started a church in Mill Woods, was killed May 11, 2014, when a utility trailer became detached from the pickup that was pulling it, causing the trailer to veer into oncoming traffic and strike Nsengiyumva's car on Airport Road.

EDMONTON - It takes a special determination to start a new church in a new country.

And it takes a special determination to adopt seven orphaned children in Africa and secure their future in Canada.

Cyprien Nsengiyumva had that determination. Despite formidable obstacles, the 43-year-old native of Burundi came to Canada, welcomed his extended family, started a church, and was starting to see the congregation flourish.

He was killed in a collision on Airport Road near Nisku Sunday, when a flatbed utility trailer became detached from the pickup that was pulling it, veered into oncoming traffic, and struck the car Nsengiyumva was driving.

"He was a man full of hope. Cyprien did not care if a situation was really bad. He was a person with special skills to deal with distress," said his wife of almost 20 years, Marie-Goretti Niyakire on Friday. The couple has four children.

"So, it didn't matter how (our) church started with no one, he was full of hope this ministry is going to grow,

and that he is going to impact the Canadian community."

Nsengiyumva was a quiet and well-liked man in his community, with some saying that "not even the devil" had a problem with him. His wife recalls that in their home country, many people — even adults — called him "muyomba," which means maternal uncle. "In my community, when someone is called muyomba it is to respect and honour. Everyone called him muyomba, muyomba," Niyakire said.

Nsengiyumva was born in Burundi and had a strong Christian faith since childhood. He was ordained a pastor in Burundi on May 11, 2003 — exactly nine years before he would be killed on an Alberta highway.

When the couple moved to Canada, Nsengiyumva's wife came first with their children in 2004. Nsengiyumva was still working in Burundi when his sister and her husband were killed, leaving behind their seven children. Nsengiyumva, of course, took them in.

"He travelled, a road trip, from Burundi to Nairobi, which is a very long trip with seven children, and he

cared for them alone, a man with seven children. And not only that, he didn't stop. He advocated on behalf of them at the Nairobi Canadian Embassy until they were accepted to come to Canada as sponsored immigrants."

After the children came to Canada and settled into jobs and school and families, Nsengiyumva would say it was his "great joy" to see them succeed.

Once in Canada, Nsengiyumva graduated to become a licensed practical nurse. The family attended different churches but Nsengiyumva could see the need for a church to serve members of the African community. Nsengiyumva had been attending the Beaumont Community Church, and with their mentorship he started the New Life Christian Fellowship in Mill Woods.

At the first service, the only people in attendance were Nsengiyumva and his family. But over the last two years, attendance has grown to about 50 people, with parts of the service done in English, French, Swahili, and Kirundi.

"He was burdened to start a church where he would be able to minister in the language people are comfortable with," his wife said.

Leduc RCMP say they are still investigating the collision to determine whether the trailer was properly hitched to the pickup.

azabjek@edmontonjournal.com

Used with permission from Edmonton Journal.

CHAPTER 16
My Heroes

My parents and my siblings are my heroes. My father didn't have a chance to finish high school. He was born in 1945 and got married in 1967; he was 22 years old when he married my mom. He passed away at 53 years old in 1998.

My mother was 16 years old when they got married. She was born in 1952 and went to be with the Lord when she was 51 years old, in 2003.

My dad and mom didn't go to school because their parents chose for them to look after livestock. This was popular in their villages because they didn't know the importance of going to school.

My dad moved to Bujumbura, the capital city of Burundi in 1966. He was 21years old. Both my mom and dad were born in the village of Matana in Bururu, one of the Burundian Provinces.

My dad later moved to the capital city, Bujumbura in 1966, where he started making a living by selling clothes. He knew my mom; they were born in the same village. But it is when he returned to the village for a visit in his twenties that he had a desire to marry her. My mom was still living in the village because she was born there and never left. It was her home.

My father's family didn't want him to marry my mom because they thought she was too young. My dad didn't waste any time listening to them. He told them: "I love her, and I have to marry her." My mother chose to marry my father because she loved him as well. They were in love. So they married, and at the beginning it was very hard for my mother, not being loved by my father's family.

A few months after my parents got married, my mom ended up having a baby girl named Beatrice. However, Beatrice died after a few months. My mother didn't get pregnant again for three years. That was one of the worst things that could happen to a woman in those days.

After three years of marriage, my dad decided to move with her to Bujumbura. He thought it would be best for my mom after everything she had been through with the loss of their baby and the way she was being mistreated.

My parents worked their businesses all their lives. Sometimes their business went down because of the war, but they didn't give up. Only twice did they stop doing business: after the war in Rwanda in 1994 and when my mom went to jail in 2001.

My Mother's Sacrifice

The rebels who took my mom's life asked her, "Where are your kids?" She answered that we were on vacation when we were in the same house hiding under the bed. Mom was a hero. We could have died with her. She saved the life of everyone who was in the house that night. From where we were hiding, we could hear our mom begging them, "Please don't kill me!" but they didn't have any mercy, nor did they feel sorry for her. She asked if they could at least kill her outside and not in her house. So they took her with my sister Florence and niece Uwizeye who were in the same room when the rebels entered our house. Florence later told us that they were making fun of our mother, that they were physically and emotionally abusive to her.

They got to a place about five kilometers away from our house, stopped and made my mom sit down while Florence and Uwizeye were still there. They kept mocking her, asking about her ethnic background and which political party she was with. She answered that she wasn't with any political party and that she was Burundian. They got very upset because they didn't get the answers they wanted. Then they tried to abuse Florence sexually but mom begged them not to do such a thing to her daughter. They finally let my sister and niece go and told them to go tell others what they saw. Florence and Uwizeye left, but they didn't know where to go since it was the middle of the night. They knocked on someone's door and were welcomed in since they were only young girls. In the morning we saw Florence and Uwizeye coming towards where we were hiding in the bushes. We asked them how our mom was doing, and they told us she was okay, because when they had left the area, our mom was still alive. It is later that a friend came to tell us that our mom had been killed.

We could not believe it. We were in shock. Mom was the only person we could look at and see a future; we couldn't see any kind of future without her. She was the most reliable, hardest working person I ever met. Moreover, she always put other people first. She loved her children more than anything, and she would have done anything just for us to be safe. My mother accepted to die alone to save her children's lives. I'll express it again; my mom was a true hero. She sacrificed her life to protect her children. She saved the life of everyone who was in the house that night, the darkest hour of my life, a night that I will never forget. May God forgive those who hurt and killed my mother.

When my mom was in Rwanda 1993, she came to get us right after she heard about all the violence and killing that was going on because of the death of the president, Melchior Ndadaye. She came straight to Burundi to get us and took us back to Rwanda. She didn't care about how dangerous it was for her to travel to reach us; the safety of her children was her priority.

When my sister Georgette had run away with our aunt, mom went to bring her back from the refugee camp so that she could be with the rest of the family. I had a brave mother.

I would also describe my mother as beautiful, giving, nurturing, thoughtful, loving, patient, kind, generous, forgiving, energetic, hard-working, and determined. She was the best mom anyone could ever want.

My mother was the true definition of a mother – completely selfless, in a way that she would literally sacrifice her life for us, and she did just that. She was a great mom, wonderful friend and a good neighbor; everyone simply adored her. Every time she would come home from work, all the neighborhood children would run over to hug and kiss her; this is how much she was loved and honored.

I cannot touch nor see my mom anymore, but she lives in my heart forever.

My mother's name was Capitoline Nikundana, also known as "Mama Richard." My father's name was Ndabaneze Manasse. They were the best parents anyone could ever ask for.

When the war began in Burundi in 1972, my dad passed through the Democratic Republic of Congo and continued till he reached Rwanda. My mom stayed in Burundi wondering what to do, not knowing if she would ever see her husband again. She was with my older brother Richard who was a baby at the time.

There was a man who helped my dad escape to Rwanda, and when they arrived, he robbed my dad and went back to Burundi. On his way back to Burundi, the man ran into my mom. She asked him if he knew where my dad was. When the man answered that he did, my mom begged him to take her to my dad, and the man accepted.

It was a long walk from Burundi to Congo. Along the way, my mother ran into problems. Some men wanted to rape her, not having any concern for the little boy she was carrying. But by God's protection, they were unsuccessful, and my mom and the man continued walking. It took them a few days to get to Rwanda. When they were getting closer, the man began to think that my dad might seek revenge for having robbed him, although I doubt my dad would've done anything to hurt him. Instead, I think my dad would have been grateful towards him for bringing his wife to him. Nonetheless, the man disappeared, and my mom couldn't find him anymore.

My mother and her baby were left alone, not knowing where to go and what to do. She started asking Rwandan people if they knew any Burundian people in the area. She finally found a Burundian family and asked them if they knew my dad, and fortunately, they did. The Burundian family then went to inform my dad that his wife was in Rwanda, and my dad came to get her.

Our parents used to tell us how they lived in poverty in Rwanda; they could barely eat, and the baby got sick because of malnutrition. That's when they got the idea of starting a business in Rwanda, where they were earning fifty cents per day. Back in those days that was a lot of money. They didn't give up; they continued with the business, and it grew. As a result, my mother and father became well known all over our small town.

Our parents were both known as selfless people. When I was growing up, our house was like a boarding school. We were fourteen children in the family, but in the house, there were more than that because many people would send their children to live with us. People knew how nice our parents were and that everyone was treated equally. My parents had fourteen children, but during this time, we never lacked anything. We were well taken care of; we even wore beautiful clothes. I remember the day I got hit in the head and lost my finger, I was wearing cute clothes. Even the nurses were talking about our clothing, concluding we were from a wealthy family by the quality of what we were wearing. Even though our clothes were covered in blood, people could tell they were new and expensive.

Despite the fact that our family fled from one country to another due to the war, and at times we were left behind, our parents worked hard for us to be happy and to have a good life.

There is one particular thing my mom did that I will never forget; she did a lot for us, but this one touched my heart in a unique way.

When we had left Burundi for Congo, it was because of the ongoing war, during which we were not able to sleep at night due to the sound of gunshots, continually having to be alert and ready to run at any time of the day or night. When we got to Congo, our father could no longer work, so our mother made the decision to go back to the war-zone of Burundi to make a living while the rest of us stayed in Congo with our father. He wasn't able to work anymore because of a problem with his leg. So my mom worked in Burundi, the same place we had left because of the war. She sacrificed herself for my siblings and me staying in an unsafe location just to make sure we had food on the table.

Even though she was working hard, it was challenging to come back to Congo and bring us money to survive. The soldiers at the Congo border would search her down to her underwear looking for money. They would even search her brassiere thinking that money was in there. I remember mom telling us that she had ripped and sown her shoes to hide her money inside and wore them across the border. Thankfully they never checked her shoes.

Both our parents were terrific. Having our father around, we were fully protected because he would do anything to make sure we were safe, even with a broken leg. No one would try to touch his children as he was very protective.

I remember when I was young, people used to remind my dad that his wife did not give him enough boys, that he had too many girls. They tried to convince him to leave her and marry someone else, but my dad would not listen to them. He stayed with my mom, and they had fourteen children – ten girls and four boys. My dad did not see the difference between girls and boys and always treated us all the same.

In those days, having boys was critical, because boys would stay with their parents while girls went to live somewhere else with their husbands. Boys would also inherit from their parents while girls would get their own land with their husbands. Parents treated boys and girls differently. Boys received more schooling than girls. Parents focused much more on their boys because they were taught that boys had more of a future than girls. As such, when we lost our parents, nobody wanted to take care of us. They wanted boys. Another reason why people wanted boys rather than girls was because girls could get pregnant before marriage, which would bring shame to the family and their friends.

In 1998, after the death of my father, many people were surprised to see a single mother such as my mom raise us alone. We had a big car that our parents had bought together. My mother worked hard and was able to buy a second car on her own. She was doing all of that for her children to have a good life. We truly had the most excellent parents.

My Siblings

My siblings mean the world to me because we were there for each other through all the ups and downs that we experienced growing up together. They are the only ones who can really understand me and I would do anything to bring a smile to their faces. As we have gotten older, my siblings and I have gotten closer. The unconditional love and support we have for one another is like no other relationship. It may seem like a cliché, but I know firsthand that there is nothing as unique as the bond between siblings, and as for me there is nothing that can break that bond. We may fight about one thing or another, but we would never allow anything to create distance between us. My relationship with my siblings is one of the most important and meaningful aspects of my life. If there was a life lesson I feel I could teach someone, it would be never to take that bond for granted.

CHAPTER 17
My Schooling

"But he said to me, 'My grace is sufficient for you, for my power is made perfect in weakness.' Therefore I will boast all the more gladly about my weaknesses, so that Christ's power may rest on me."
(2 Corinthians 12:9 NIV)

I started grade one when I was five years old. My older sister went to school, and I followed her. She and I were very close. I just couldn't see myself staying home. Her teacher didn't like it because I was under the required age to go to school. He started sending me back, and I cried all the way to our house. Some of the days, I was hiding in the classroom while class was happening. My parents decided to go to school and talk to the teacher, but my sister's teacher still refused to take me in.

We moved to Kigali, Rwanda because of the war and that's when I started kindergarten. Everything was great; I was a brilliant child. When I was about to go into grade one, that's when president Ndadaye was elected in Burundi, and our parents sent everyone who was in school to Burundi. In Burundi, I was in grade one for a few months, and President Ndadaye was killed. My mom then came and took us back to Rwanda.

A few months after finishing grade one, the year was 1994, and they killed the president of Rwanda, Habyarimana. That's when we went to Congo and spent one year in the refugee camp. There was no school and no education for us there. Life was tough for us there and that's when our parents decided to take us to Burundi. In Burundi, they put me in grade two. I couldn't understand the teaching in Kirundi.

In Rwanda, we spoke Kinyarwanda and were taught in Kinyarwanda, but in Burundi, they spoke Kirundi and were trained in Kirundi and in French. At that time in Burundi, French was introduced in grade one while in Rwanda, it was only taught from grade four onward.

The war in Burundi was never-ending; while I was in grade two, that's when we ran and stayed in the bush for few months. By God's grace, we were able to leave that area and end up in Mugara, Rumonge. In Mugara, I was put into grade three, and in the middle of that school year, my parents decided to go back to Congo. They tried so hard for us to have a better life.

In Congo, I went into grade three once more. My education became very hard. I went from being taught in Kinyarwanda to being taught in Kirundi, and in

Congo, the school was in French and Swahili. I couldn't understand a thing.

In Congo, I recall that they had a system in place for finding people who couldn't speak French. During break, anyone who couldn't utter French went to hide themselves. They had a book where they to put the names of everyone who spoke other languages. After break, they gave that book to the teacher and those whose names were on the list were to be caned by the teacher.

I repeated grade three in Congo. At the beginning of the following school year in October, that's when the war began in Congo, and we were forced to go back to Burundi. In Burundi, I went to school in Rukaramu and was put into grade three again. Because of the war, every year I was in a different school. I spent grade four in Matana, Bururi, after the death of my father. It is after that time that I spent one year at home and in the hospital after becoming ill.

I then spent grade five through grade nine in different schools in Burundi and grade ten and eleven in Kenya. Then we came to Canada in 2006.

It's in Canada that I decided to learn English. I went to St. Francis in Edmonton for the Language Instruction for Newcomers to Canada (LINC) program for one year. Then I got transferred to the

English as a Second Language (ESL) program for one year at NorQuest College.

After that, I decided to take the Heath Care Aid program for one year at NorQuest College. And in 2009, I moved to Ottawa.

In Ottawa, I decided to go back to school to get my high school diploma. I went to Rochester Adult High School and continued to St. Nicholas Adult High School where I got my high school diploma. It was complicated to keep changing schools throughout my life, but I didn't have a choice. And I got to experience firsthand God's promise that His grace is sufficient, and that His strength is perfected in weakness (2 Corinthians 12:9).

I will continue with my studies; I will not stop where I am. My plan is to go to University and obtain a degree.

CONCLUSION

"Be strong and courageous. Do not be afraid or terrified because of them, for the LORD your God goes with you; he will never leave you nor forsake you."
(Deuteronomy 31:6 NIV)

Our God will never leave you nor forsake you (Deuteronomy 31:6); don't give up on Him. Just as He was there for me through it all, He is also right there with you. When I was young, I used to hear preachers say, "God is the Father of the fatherless and protector of widows." (Psalm 68:5 ESV) It didn't make sense to me at the time, but I understood it when I lost my parents, and had nowhere to go. I couldn't see my future as a young girl, but I saw God as my father.

After God saved our lives and brought us to Canada, we neither suffered from hunger nor homelessness. God sent our uncle to take care of us. For a man to accept to take on seven children on top of his own three was very unusual and undoubtedly God at work in his heart. God did not leave my siblings and me; He was always there for us.

I would like to encourage someone who is going through hardship to have faith in God. You may not have food, shelter or even water to drink, or you may be facing challenges that seem like they will never end, but know that I was once like you. God will turn your pain to happiness. You can hold onto His promise that He will turn your mourning into dancing: "You turned my wailing into dancing; you removed my sackcloth and clothed me with joy." (Psalm 30:11 NIV) The Bible also says, "Weeping may last through the night, but joy comes with the morning." (Psalm 30:5 ESV)

You may not see how this could be true at this present moment, but if you hold on to His Word, it shall surely come to pass in your life.

You might also be facing the loss of a loved one, but know that even in your heartache, God is with you. When you go through hard times, do not blame God. Instead, take time to thank God for what you have and who He is.

I remember when I was bleeding all over my head, and my two hands were in so much pain from shielding myself from the rebels trying to kill me; even when I was told that my parents and siblings had died, I refused to blame God. Instead, I looked at how my sister and I survived, and I was grateful for that. Keep praying and worshiping Him, and He will surprise you.

I would like to end with the topic of forgiveness. My Pastor often speaks of the importance of forgiving one another. I thank God because with everything I've been through, forgiving others has become the easiest thing for me to do in my life. I have forgiven everyone who ever wronged me. I have nothing hidden inside my heart.

People may have hurt you severely, and it may be difficult for you to forgive them, but you can take it from me that by forgiving others, you will find rest for your soul. And by ridding your heart of the bitterness and pain that comes from the inability to forgive, you will leave room for joy and freedom to inhabit your heart again. If I can forgive, so can you.

"Forget the former things; do not dwell on the past. See, I am doing a new thing! Now it springs up; do you not perceive it? I am making a way in the wilderness and streams in the wasteland."
(Isaiah 43:18-19 NIV)

10098909R00055

Manufactured by
Amazon.ca
Bolton, ON